# CHINA
## Land, Life, and Culture

## Wildlife

JOHN AND JACKIE TIDEY

**Marshall Cavendish**
Benchmark

New York

This edition first published in 2009 in the United States of America by Marshall Cavendish Benchmark.

Marshall Cavendish Benchmark
99 White Plains Road
Tarrytown, NY 10591
www.marshallcavendish.us

First published in 2008 by
MACMILLAN EDUCATION AUSTRALIA PTY LTD
15–19 Claremont Street, South Yarra 3141

Visit our website at www.macmillan.com.au or go directly to www.macmillanlibrary.com.au

Associated companies and representatives throughout the world.

Copyright © John and Jackie Tidey 2008

Library of Congress Cataloging-in-Publication Data

Tidey, John.
  Wildlife / by John and Jackie Tidey.
    p. cm. — (China—land, life, and culture)
  ISBN 978-0-7614-3161-9
  1. Animals—China—Juvenile literature.  I. Tidey, Jackie.  II. Title.
  QL307.T53 2008
591.951—dc22
                                        2008002853

Edited by Georgina Garner
Text and cover design by Peter Shaw
Page layout by Peter Shaw
Photo research by Jes Senbergs
Maps by Damien Demaj, DEMAP

Printed in the United States

**Acknowledgments**
The author and the publisher are grateful to the following for permission to reproduce copyright material:

Cover photograph: giant pandas, by Alex Headley

AAP Images/AP Photo/Xinhua, Zhang Guojun, **16**; Gary Ades, **29** (top); Alamy, **8**; Auscape International Photo Library/Peter Arnold, **15** (middle left); Auscape International Photo Library/Jean-Paul Ferrero, **15** (top left), **19** (bottom); Auscape International Photo Library/Nature Production, **20**; Auscape International Photo Library/ Oxford Scientific Films, **11**; Marion Ducco, **4** (top right); Getty Images, **3** (top left), **7** (bottom), **9, 10, 12, 14** (both), **15** (top right, bottom left & bottom right), **19** (top), **21, 22, 23** (top middle, bottom left & bottom right), **26, 27, 30** (top & bottom); Minden Pictures/Getty Images, **28** (right); Alex Headley, **1, 5** (top), **6**; Doug Hendrie, **29** (middle & bottom); © istockphoto.com, **4** (bottom left); © Ying Chen/istockphoto.com, **4** (bottom right); © Jaime Roset/istockphoto.com, **3** (bottom left), **23** (top left); © Christopher Waters/istockphoto.com, **23** (top right); Memphis Zoo, **28** (left); © Peter E. Smith, Natural Sciences Image Library, **18** (bottom); PhotoDisc/Alan & Sandy Carey, **5** (bottom); © Shutterstock, **24** (insert), **25** (bottom); © Max FX/Shutterstock, **4** (bottom middle), **30**; © Jozsef Szasz-Fabian/Shutterstock, **24** (main & insert); © Thomas Peter Voss/Shutterstock, **3** (top right), **13**; James Wu, **4** (top left & top middle), **17, 18** (top); WWF, **7** (right).

1 3 5 6 4 2

# Contents

## Glossary Words

When a word is printed in **bold**, you can look up its meaning in the Glossary on page 31.

## Chinese Proverb

*Once on the tiger's back, it is difficult to get off.*

# China, A Big Country

China challenges the imagination because of its size. It is big in many ways. It is one of the largest countries on Earth, covering about one-fifth of the continent of Asia. China's population of more than 1.3 billion, or 1,300,000,000, is the world's largest. It has an ancient civilization and a recorded history that date back thousands of years.

A large area of China is covered by tall mountains and wide deserts. Most of the population lives in the fertile lowlands that are bordered by the Pacific Ocean in the east.

## The People's Republic of China

Today, China is formally known as the People's Republic of China (P.R.C.). In the last thirty years, the P.R.C. have gone through great social change and the **economy** has grown enormously. China is now one of the United States' major trading partners.

This book features many of the abundant forms of wildlife in China. These include the well-known giant panda, the pheasants of Sichuan, and the elusive snow leopard of the mountains.

An ancient history

Traditional arts

Very old customs

A country of extremes

A rich variety of wildlife

Plants and medicinal herbs

# Diversity of Wildlife

China is a country with great **biodiversity**. There are more than 4,400 **species** of **vertebrates** and more than 100 of these species are unique to China. The most well-known of these animals is the giant panda.

The giant panda is one of China's national treasures.

## Wildlife Conservation

Countries around the world are helping China to conserve its abundant wildlife. The giant panda is the most famous of these threatened species, but some other rare and endangered species are the golden monkey, the Chinese alligator, and the South China tiger. Sometimes, there are conflicts between the development of the economy and conservation. To help save endangered creatures, hundreds of wildlife breeding centers have been set up throughout China in the last few decades.

### For Your Information

China began building nature reserves in 1956. By 2010, the government plans to have 1,800 nature reserves. These reserves will be managed by forest authorities. They will protect wild animals, botanical species, and natural forests.

The North China leopard is endangered and very rarely seen in the wild.

# Giant Pandas

The giant panda is a beloved animal in China. It is regarded as a national treasure. It is found mostly in southwestern China in Sichuan, Shaanxi, and Gansu provinces.

The giant panda is part of the bear family. It has a white coat with black trimmings around its eyes and on its ears, arms, and legs. Adult pandas can be 5 feet (1.5 meters) long and weigh up to 330 pounds (150 kilograms).

## Behavior and Diet

The giant panda leads a solitary life, except during the mating season. It lives in bamboo forests in the mountains. It can climb trees but lives mainly on the ground. Unlike most bears, the giant panda does not **hibernate**. It moves to low-lying areas during the winter in search of warmer temperatures.

The giant panda has a mainly vegetarian diet, eating mostly bamboo shoots and leaves. It also eats insects and small **rodents**. Giant panda breeding groups are small and isolated from one another.

### Did You Know?

To meet its energy needs, an adult giant panda must eat up to 80 pounds (38 kg) of bamboo each day.

Giant pandas have bamboo for breakfast in a reserve in Sichuan Province.

# Declining Populations

Giant panda numbers have been declining for thousands of years due to:

- climate change
- loss of habitat
- **poaching**
- hunting

Some young pandas are hunted and eaten by leopards. A major study completed in 2004 estimated the population of giant pandas in the wild to be about 1,600.

In recent years, a huge international effort has been made to locate and protect giant pandas and their habitats. Breeding programs in zoos have meant that the number of giant pandas born in zoos has tripled since 2000. Late in 2006, China's foremost expert on the giant panda declared that it was no longer threatened with extinction. "I think I can say the giant panda is safe," said Zhang Hemin, head of the China Research and Conservation Center for the Giant Panda.

This newborn panda cub was bred at a research center in Sichuan Province.

## For Your Information

Around the world, the giant panda is a very well-known symbol of the fight to protect and conserve wildlife. A giant panda is used as the logo of the organization the World Wildlife Fund (WWF). The WWF has used the panda logo since the organization first started in 1961.

**WWF**

# Golden Monkeys

Golden monkeys belong to a family of monkeys called snub-nosed monkeys. Three species of these monkeys live in the mountains and forests of southern China, in Sichuan, Yunnan, and Guizhou provinces.

China's golden monkeys are endangered. Their soft fur is highly valued by poachers. The monkey's fur is so long that when it leaps from tree to tree it seems to have wings.

## Behavior and Diet

Golden monkeys live in groups of up to six hundred, but break into much smaller groups in the winter. Males and females make different calls and members of the same group "sing" together.

Golden monkeys live in the trees, but they also spend a lot of time on the ground. They have a varied diet that includes bamboo shoots, insects, small birds, pine needles, and fruits.

Golden monkeys are also called snub-nosed monkeys because of their upturned noses.

### Did You Know?

Some Chinese people believe that golden monkey fur wards off rheumatism, which causes pain in muscles and joints.

The golden monkey is the focus of the biggest species protection program in China.

# Survival

The golden monkey is endangered. It has many enemies, and poaching and habitat loss are high on the list of threats to its survival. In the past, golden monkeys were killed for their fur and for their bones, which are thought by some to have special medicinal powers. It is now illegal to hunt or kill golden monkeys, but this is hard to enforce because they live in such remote areas. Golden monkeys are shy and reclusive, so it is difficult to assess the number of these monkeys that survive in the wild.

# Conservation Program

The Yunnan Golden Monkey Program is the largest species protection program in China. International conservation groups work with Chinese authorities to better understand the needs of this precious monkey and to deal with some of the threats to its survival.

## For Your Information

The International Union for Conservation of Nature (IUCN) Red List of Threatened Species ranks animals according to the species' risk of extinction. Its categories are, from least to greatest risk:

- lower risk
- vulnerable
- endangered
- critically endangered
- extinct in the wild
- extinct

The golden monkey is classified as endangered.

# Takins

Another national treasure in the wilds of China is a large animal called the takin. Takins are massive creatures similar to goats. Some of them weigh well over 880 pounds (400 kg). A grown male of the species stands about 4 feet (1 m) at its shoulders. Takins are dark brown or golden in color, with short, curled horns and moose-like faces.

Sturdy legs and wide hooves help a takin to climb.

## Behavior and Diet

Takins are slow and careful animals that are found in mountainous country, often above the **tree line**. They are **herbivores** that feed in the early morning or late afternoon. They eat **deciduous** leaves, grasses, twigs, and even the tough leaves of **evergreen** rhododendrons. Takins are usually safe from other animal predators because they are big and live in herds. Sometimes, they can fall prey to packs of wild dogs. Takins are classified as vulnerable by the IUCN because of over-hunting and habitat destruction.

# Snow Leopards

The snow leopard that lives in the mountains of western China is a sleek, spotted cat. It shares its name with the common leopard but it is not closely related to it. The snow leopard is also found outside China, across the mountainous regions of central Asia. It is endangered because it has been hunted for its fur and bones. The fur of the snow leopard is long and soft and provides protection from the cold mountain climate.

## Behavior and Diet

One of the distinguishing features of the snow leopard is its spotted tail, which can be up to 3 feet (1 m) long. Its tail helps the animal keep its balance in snowy, uneven **terrain**. The snow leopard can wrap its long tail around itself to keep warm.

Snow leopards prey on goats, small game, rodents, and domestic livestock. They sometimes ambush their victims by leaping on them from above.

**Did You Know?**

The snow leopard is sometimes called the ounce.

The snow leopard's thick tail, long fur, and large paws mean it is well-suited to cold, snowy environments.

# South China Tigers

The South China tiger is one of six types, or subspecies, of tiger in the world. It is very close to extinction. This critically endangered animal was officially declared a pest for a short time about fifty years ago, and it was hunted almost out of existence. Now this cat is so rare in the wild that little is known about its habits. By 2006, there had been no sighting of the animal in its natural habitat for many years. There are about sixty South China tigers in zoos around the world.

## Behavior and Diet

Although little is known about the South China tiger, we do know that it is one of the smaller tiger subspecies, growing to about 8 feet (2½ m) in length. Its prey includes wild pigs, deer, antelope, and other ungulates, or hoofed animals, that it encounters. The South China tiger leads a solitary existence, except during the mating season. If it still survives in the wild, it is likely to be in the forests and grasslands of central and eastern China.

### For Your Information

The tiger is a species of the cat family. It has eight known subspecies. Two of these became extinct in the last hundred years. Six subspecies remain, all of them in Asia. All surviving subspecies are seriously threatened by habitat loss and poaching.

The six remaining subspecies are:
- the South China tiger
- the Sumatran tiger
- the Bengal tiger
- the Indo-Chinese tiger
- the Malayan tiger
- the Siberian, or Amur, tiger

These two South China tigers are kept in captivity on a wildlife reserve.

# Elephants

Elephants once roamed across most of China. Today, they are reduced to small numbers found in the southwest of the country. They are a protected species. A few years ago, Chinese authorities estimated the number of wild elephants in the country to be about 250 and growing. The largest population of Asian elephants in the world is in India.

Asian elephants are very good swimmers.

## Behavior and Diet

The Asian elephant lives in forests. China's elephants are found only in the south of Yunnan Province near the border with Laos and Burma.

In the fight for food and land resources, elephants often raid crops and sometimes even kill or injure people who get in their way.

**Did You Know?**

Elephants are the world's largest living land animals. Some weigh as much as 15,000 pounds (7,000 kg).

# Desert and Grassland Animals

China's spreading deserts occupy about 30 percent of the country. They are home to many rare and endangered creatures. The Taklimakan, one of the world's largest shifting-sands deserts, is China's largest and driest desert. There is little biodiversity in the harsh, dry desert and very little vegetation, but some animals do call the deserts of China home. The grasslands at the edges of the great deserts also support many animals.

## Bactrian Camel

The wild Bactrian camel is a well-known desert animal. For thousands of years, this two-humped camel has been a "beast of burden," carrying up to 880 pounds (400 kg) on its back. It is also the source of meat, hides, and fiber used for items such as rope and fine cloth. The Bactrian camel has adapted well to weather conditions ranging from freezing cold to extremely hot. It is considered critically endangered in the wild.

The Bactrian camel grows a thick, shaggy coat in winter.

**Did You Know?**

Bactrian camels have very tough mouths. This enables them to eat thorny bushes in the desert.

The male Mongolian gazelle has curled horns that grow up to 16 inches (40 centimeters) long.

## Mongolian Gazelle

The Mongolian gazelle is a native of the grasslands in China's northeastern region. The males have horns that curve backward from the forehead. The females do not have horns. During the mating season, males develop a swollen throat. In recent years, the number of Mongolian gazelles has dropped because of harsh weather and habitat loss.

14

# The Gobi

The Gobi Desert reaches across central Asia, covering large areas of China and Mongolia. It is one of the world's great desert regions, although much of it is not sandy, but covered with bare rock.

## Inhabitants Of the Gobi

### Ibex
The ibex is a wild mountain goat. It is good at climbing. The male has long curved horns and the female has shorter horns.

### Takhi
The takhi has been called the last true wild horse. It is also known as Przewalski's horse, after an early Russian explorer of China.

### Jerboa
The jerboa is a small, nocturnal desert creature that looks like a mouse. It can jump more than 6.5 feet (2 m).

### Golden eagle
The golden eagle is among the largest and most powerful of the raptors, or birds of prey. Its main food in the Gobi is the jerboa.

### Wild ass
The wild ass is an ancestor of today's domestic ass. It can outrun most of its predators by reaching speeds of up to 40 miles (65 kilometers) per hour.

# Ocean and River Creatures

There are thousands of marine species in the Bohai, Yellow, East China, and South China seas of the Pacific Ocean. At least 150 of these species are fished commercially by the Chinese. There are also as many as seven hundred freshwater species in China's rivers and lakes.

## Chinese Sturgeon

The Chinese sturgeon is an ancient species of fish that can grow to be 13 feet (4 m) long. It has lived in the Yangtze River and the Pearl River for around 140 million years. Mature, adult fish enter the rivers from the East China Sea and South China Sea. They migrate upstream where they spawn, or produce more sturgeon.

The Chinese sturgeon is sometimes called the "giant panda of the water" because it is critically endangered. Pollution, dams, and river traffic have wiped out many of these fish. They are now strictly protected by the Chinese government. Many breeding and protection programs have been established.

### For Your Information

Only fifty years ago, there were thousands of *baiji*, or Yangtze river dolphins, in the Yangtze River. These shy creatures were declared a national treasure. Sadly, by 2007, they were assumed to be extinct due to water pollution, fishing nets, and river accidents.

Many Chinese sturgeons are bred in captivity and released into rivers in China.

This Chinese alligator lives in a nature reserve near Shanghai.

# Chinese Alligator

The Chinese alligator is found in northeastern China, living in freshwater rivers, streams, lakes, and swamps. Their diet is varied and includes fish, clams, snails, small birds, and mammals. They grow to about 6.5 feet (2 m) in length. Scientists say they are secretive and solitary.

One local name for this alligator means "dragon." Some people think that the mythical Chinese dragon might, in fact, have been the Chinese alligator.

The Chinese alligator is one of only two alligator species in the world. The other is the American alligator. There are plenty of Chinese alligators in captivity, but they are considered critically endangered in the wild.

# Chinese Paddlefish

Imagine a very large freshwater fish with a long snout like a cone or paddle. This is what the rare Chinese paddlefish looks like. This fish is considered critically endangered.

The Chinese paddlefish can reach 6.5 feet (2 m) in length but there have been reports of some that were much larger than this. In the past, the paddlefish was common in the middle and lower sections of the Yangtze.

## For Your Information

The only other paddlefish in the world is found in North America, where it is the oldest surviving animal species.

# Birds

China is home to about 1,200 species of birds. China's vast range of territory, climate, and landscape provides homes for a wide variety of birds. In addition to the mountain, forest, and desert habitats, there are also important habitats in lakes and various types of wetlands. As a result, temperate birds, cold-climate birds, seabirds, desert birds, and tropical birds are all found in China.

## Caged Birds

Groups of men with birds in cages are a common sight on the streets of Chinese cities. They take the birds out to "air" them each morning. The cages are covered with a cloth until they get to the park or meeting place. In China, birdsong is said to lift the spirits.

These men show their birds in Penglai Park, in Shanghai.

## Mountain Pheasants

A pheasant is a large, forest-living bird that is often hunted for food. Many of the world's species of pheasant are found in the mountains of Sichuan Province. The plumage, or feathers, of the male pheasant is more colorful and elaborate than that of the female. One of the most distinctive of these birds is the Lady Amherst's pheasant and another is the Temminck's tragopan. For hundreds of years, Temminck's tragopan was trapped and caged because it was thought to bring its owners long life, wealth, and success.

The male Lady Amherst's pheasant has colorful plumage.

18

There are believed to be only about forty-eight crested ibis left in the wild in China.

# The Crested Ibis

The crested ibis is one of the rarest birds in the world. It was once common in Japan, where it is known as the Japanese crested ibis, as well as in Korea, Russia, and China. There are a small number left in the wild in southern China. There are several reasons for the decline of the crested ibis, such as habitat loss, hunting, and the effect of pesticides. The crested ibis is considered critically endangered. Breeding programs in nature reserves and research centers have been established in China and Japan.

# Red-Crowned Crane

China's red-crowned crane is famous for its graceful courtship dance and for the fact that it is the only crane species that has white outer-wing feathers. It stands up to 5 feet (1.5 m) tall. Cranes have a special place in Chinese culture and history. About half of the world's species of cranes are found in China.

The red-crowned crane is considered endangered. Habitat destruction is the main threat to its survival. The International Crane Foundation is a scientific organization that works toward the preservation of crane species around the world.

A red-crowned crane is seen as a sign of long life and immortality in Taoist philosophy.

# Butterflies and Moths

Butterflies and moths make up one animal family, called *Lepidoptera.* The silkworm moth is the most well known of all China's butterflies and moths. The Chinese butterfly with the highest level of state protection is called the Golden Kaiser-e-Hind. It gets its name from the golden marks on its hind wings.

The Chinese yellow swallowtail butterfly is found in eastern China.

## "Kingdom of Butterflies"

Yunnan Province has a long history of flower-growing and is known as the "Kingdom of Flowers." It has also been called the "Kingdom of Butterflies," or "flowers that can fly." Yunnan Province is home to more than seven hundred species of butterfly. China's first butterfly museum was built near the city of Kunming, in Yunnan Province.

## Powerful Symbols

Although fragile animals, butterflies have had powerful symbolic meaning since ancient times. They are strong symbols in China, representing joy, transformation, and freedom, among other things. There is a famous Chinese legend about a tragic romance that is called *The Butterfly Lovers.*

**Did You Know?**

The butterfly has a very short life. On average, it lives for just a few weeks.

# Bees

The bee has a long and interesting history in China. The bee was **domesticated** in ancient China, so that the Chinese could collect honey and beeswax.

Honey has long been regarded as a source of food and energy. China is now the largest honey-producing country in the world and has more than one-third of the international market.

Beeswax is said to have been used in traditional Chinese medicine during the great Han Dynasty. Much later, it was used for candles and other objects.

There is a bee museum in Beijing today. This museum has bee fossils and rock drawings dating back more than six thousand years.

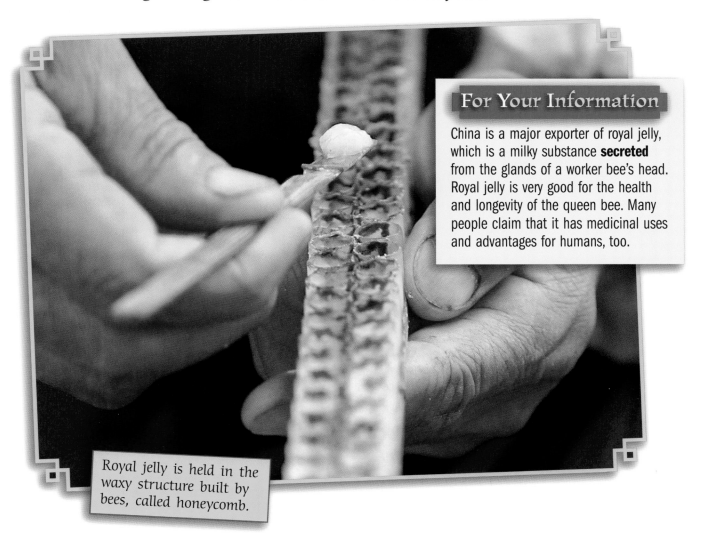

Royal jelly is held in the waxy structure built by bees, called honeycomb.

### For Your Information
China is a major exporter of royal jelly, which is a milky substance **secreted** from the glands of a worker bee's head. Royal jelly is very good for the health and longevity of the queen bee. Many people claim that it has medicinal uses and advantages for humans, too.

21

# Silkworms

For thousands of years, sericulture, or the keeping of silkworms for silk, was a well-kept secret in China. The penalty for revealing the secret that silk came from the cocoons of the silkworm was death. The Chinese first domesticated silkworms and began breeding them for silk at least five thousand years ago.

## Precious Fabric

The ancient Chinese were the first people to master the art of **weaving** silk, using strands from the cocoons of silkworms. Silk is a light, soft, and shiny fabric. It is used in many items of clothing, such as dresses, suits, ties, and scarves. Silk was beautiful and rare, so it was valued highly and considered precious.

**Did You Know?**

China is the world's largest silk producer. In 2005, it produced almost 75 percent of the world's raw silk and 90 percent of silk exports.

These women sort silkworm cocoons to make silk to sell on the Silk Road.

## The Silk Road

About two thousand years ago, a great network of trade routes opened up, linking China and other parts of Asia with Europe. This was called the Silk Road. People, goods, inventions, and ideas moved along the Silk Road, and eventually the secret of the silkworm did, too. As the secret spread far and wide, China lost its control over the silk trade.

# How Silk Is Made

1 Newly hatched silkworms eat the leaves of the white mulberry tree for a month and grow bigger. The silkworms shed their skins several times while they are eating and turn white.

2 When fully grown, the silkworms spin cocoons around themselves. The cocoons are collected and sorted by hand. Some are thrown away.

3 The best cocoons are placed in warm water and then boiled to loosen the silk strands of the cocoon.

4 A strand is taken from each of five cocoons. These strands are unwound from the cocoons and twisted together to make silk thread. The silk threads are stretched on wooden frames and dyed brilliant colors.

5 Finally, the silk threads are woven together to make silk.

# Animal Signs

Chinese animal signs are a unique system that dates the years over a twelve-year cycle. Each year in the cycle has been given an animal name, or sign, such as rat, ox, or tiger. Every twelve years the same animal name reappears.

## Astrological Signs

The idea of the twelve Chinese **astrological signs** dates back at least two thousand years. According to one **legend**, Buddha invited all the animals to join him on New Year's Day. Twelve animals turned up. As a reward, a year was named for each one, in the order that they arrived:

- rat
- ox
- tiger
- rabbit
- dragon
- snake
- horse
- sheep
- monkey
- rooster
- dog
- pig

The ox was the second to arrive at Buddha's New Year's Day celebration.

### For Your Information

The twelve astrological signs we are familiar with in the **West** are Aries, Taurus, Gemini, Cancer, Leo, Virgo, Libra, Scorpio, Sagittarius, Capricorn, Aquarius, and Pisces.

The rooster was the tenth animal to arrive at Buddha's feast.

# Chinese Horoscopes

Just as **horoscopes** developed in the West, the same happened in China. A person's astrological sign is decided by things such as the position of the Sun, Moon, and planets at the time of a person's birth. These astrological signs lead to horoscopes, or predictions.

Look through the twelve signs to see which one is your sign. While these horoscopes are fun, they should not be regarded seriously.

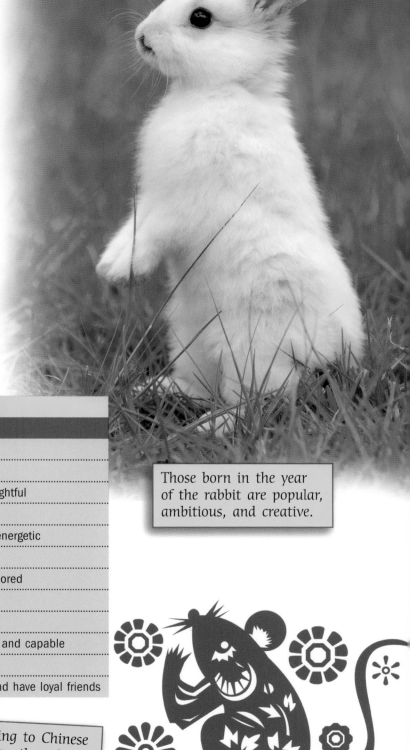

Those born in the year of the rabbit are popular, ambitious, and creative.

**Did You Know?**
The dragon was the symbol of the Chinese emperor for thousands of years.

## Chinese Astrological Signs

| Animal | Birth Years | Characteristics |
|---|---|---|
| Rat | 1984, 1996, 2008 | Clever, confident, and optimistic |
| Ox | 1985, 1997, 2009 | Quiet, patient, and stubborn |
| Tiger | 1986, 1998, 2010 | Sensitive, courageous, and thoughtful |
| Rabbit | 1987, 1999, 2011 | Popular, ambitious, and creative |
| Dragon | 1988, 2000, 2012 | Strong-minded, impatient, and energetic |
| Snake | 1989, 2001, 2013 | Wise and egotistical |
| Horse | 1990, 2002, 2014 | Well-liked and always good-humored |
| Sheep | 1991, 2003, 2015 | Thoughtful, shy, and kind |
| Monkey | 1992, 2004, 2016 | Clever, flexible, and successful |
| Rooster | 1993, 2005, 2017 | Eccentric, as well as thoughtful, and capable |
| Dog | 1994, 2006, 2018 | Loyal, discreet, and reliable |
| Pig | 1995, 2007, 2019 | Full of energy, eager to learn, and have loyal friends |

According to Chinese astrology, those born in the year of the rat are clever.

# Protecting Wildlife

China's Wildlife Protection Law prohibits illegal hunting and the destruction of wildlife resources. This law was introduced in 1998. This focus on wildlife conservation in China has attracted a great deal of international support.

## The Red List

The World Conservation Union (IUCN) publishes a list of species with rankings such as critically endangered, endangered, and vulnerable. This is called the Red List of Threatened Species. The IUCN is the largest and most important conservation network in the world. It consults widely with experts before deciding which species are considered endangered.

### For Your Information

Although the name World Conservation Union is used, the letters IUCN stand for the union's formal name, the International Union for the Conservation of Nature and Natural Resources. It has many projects in China.

China's Milu deer, or Père David's deer, are now found only on reserves and in zoos.

# Preserving Diversity

An organization called the Nature Conservancy is working to preserve the animals, plants, and natural communities that represent the diversity of life on Earth. It has projects in more than thirty countries, including China.

# Protecting Golden Monkeys

The Nature Conservancy has launched a school program to alert children to the threats faced by the rare golden monkey. Conservation volunteers dressed in golden monkey costumes visit schools in the Yunnan Province to raise awareness of the plight of these monkeys.

# Captive Population of Giant Pandas

A research center near the city of Chengdu, in Sichuan Province, is home to a large population of giant pandas bred in captivity or brought in from the wild. The center is devoted to the breeding and preservation of these famous animals. The ultimate goal is to reintroduce these giant pandas to the wild.

## For Your Information

The giant panda has been called "nature's gift" to the city of Chengdu and Sichuan Province. The local government in Chengdu wants to make the area a major tourism center by 2010.

Giant pandas play at the Wolong Giant Panda Research and Conservation Center.

# Global Survival Program

As part of an international breeding and research effort, China has loaned some of its giant pandas to zoos around the world. These pandas are in countries as far away from China as Spain and at several zoos in the United States.

## U.S. Zoos

California's San Diego Zoo says it has had a love affair with giant pandas since two of them first came to visit more than twenty years ago. Now the zoo has a giant panda research station. Some of its main research work is studying how its celebrity guests communicate.

Zoo Atlanta, in Georgia, is very interested in the reproductive and maternal behavior of its giant pandas. Nutrition is the main focus at Memphis Zoo, in Tennessee.

## Hua Mei

Hua Mei was the first giant panda born in the United States to survive to adulthood. She left San Diego Zoo and went to live in China in 2004. By 2007, Hua Mei had given birth to three sets of twins.

Hua Mei is checked by a keeper at San Diego Zoo.

Memphis Zoo in Tennessee is home to this giant panda.

# Kadoorie Farm and Botanic Garden

Kadoorie Farm and Botanic Garden is in the New Territories, in Hong Kong. It is involved in both researching and rescuing China's wildlife, and educating people about it. It also helps the Hong Kong government by caring for turtles that have been seized from poachers and sellers in the illegal wildlife trade.

## MEET Gary Ades

Gary Ades works in Hong Kong at the Kadoorie Farm and Botanic Garden (KFBG). For the past eight years, he has worked with a team of people at KFBG who are trying to save the endangered turtles of southeast Asia.

### In Conversation with Gary Ades

Several cultures in southeast Asia see turtles as part of their normal diet. Eating a few turtles at a time did not cause big problem for wild populations. Now turtles have become big business. They are farmed in great numbers or captured from rivers and then sold for food or medicine.

Thousands of turtles each day are being sold in markets all around China. Most of the turtles have been removed from the wild. Very soon some species of turtle will be gone forever.

At Kadoorie Farm we have been researching the illegal trade in turtles, rescuing the turtles, and passing them to conservation organizations around the world. We hope that they or their future offspring will one day be able to return to their natural homes in the forests and wetlands of southeast Asia and China.

These turtles are waiting to be sold in a market in China.

A turtle is caught by a fisherman.

# Conserving Diversity

From the famous giant panda to the ancient paddlefish, China has thousands of wildlife species, many of which are found only in China. Population pressures and advancing deserts are just two threats to China's wildlife. The golden monkey is at risk, along with the rare South China tiger and the snow leopard.

## A Global Fight

Countries around the world are helping China to save and develop its abundant wildlife. The giant panda has become the best known symbol of the global fight to protect and conserve all wildlife. A huge international effort was made to locate and protect the giant panda, which is now no longer threatened with extinction.

A villager in northern China plants a tree to stop the advance of the desert.

Giant pandas are being bred successfully in captivity.

A herd of wild ass graze on a grassy plain.

# Glossary

| | |
|---|---|
| astrological signs | animals or mythical figures that represent a person's birth month or year |
| biodiversity | the range of animal and plant species |
| deciduous | plants that shed their leaves annually |
| domesticated | made tame; not wild |
| economy | the finances of a country |
| evergreen | having green leaves all year round |
| herbivores | animals that feed only on plants |
| hibernate | to withdraw and remain alone during winter |
| horoscopes | the telling of the future from the study of the positions of the Sun, Moon, and planets |
| legend | a popular story that is handed down and is thought to be at least partly true |
| poaching | taking animals or fish illegally |
| rodents | animals such as rats and mice |
| secreted | separated from |
| species | groups of living things that have common characteristics |
| terrain | the natural surface features of a large piece of land |
| tree line | the point above sea level at which trees stop growing |
| vertebrates | animals that have a backbone |
| weaving | to cross threads over and under each other to form a fabric or texture |
| West | the parts of the developed world that are not covered by eastern Asia |

# Index